THE
BIG
TIME

SELENA GOMEZ

VALERIE BODDEN

"like" us on
facebook

Visit us on the web at:
www.alta.lib.ia.us
or call (712) 200-1250
to renew your books!

CREATIVE EDUCATION

SELENA GOMEZ

TABLE OF CONTENTS

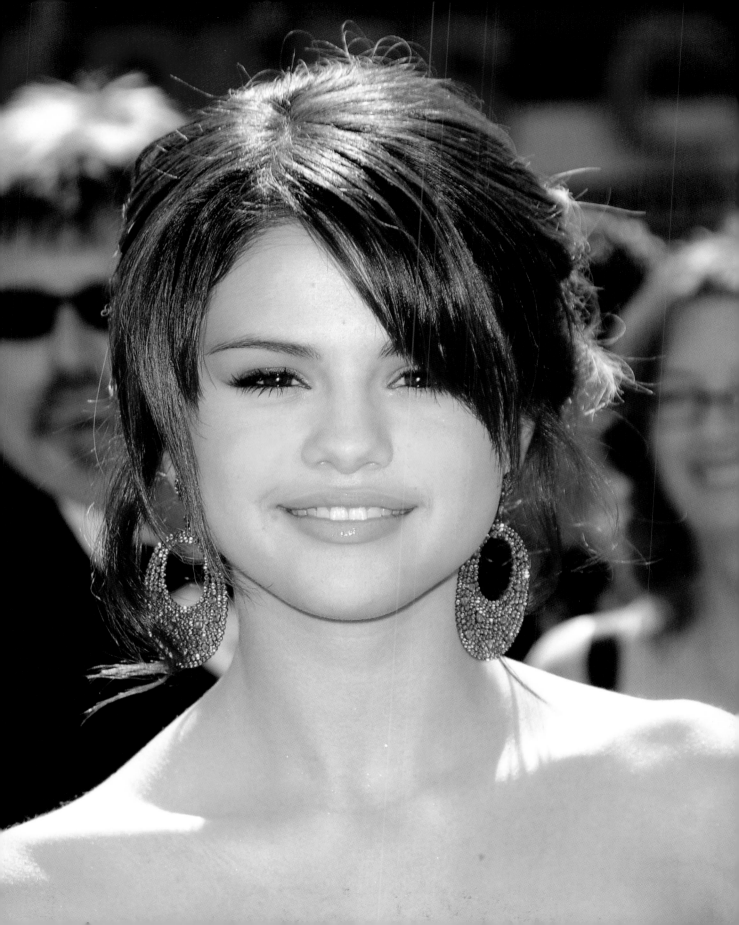

MEET SELENA

Selena stands in a recording studio. She sings the same song again and again. She wants to get it just right. Soon, she will sing the song in concert. Fans around the world will buy her new album.

Selena Gomez is an actress and singer. Fans know her for TV shows like *Wizards of Waverly Place*. They watch her in movies like *Ramona and Beezus*. And they love her music.

Selena and Joey King played sisters in the movie Ramona and Beezus *(left)*.

SELENA'S CHILDHOOD

Selena was born July 22, 1992. She grew up in Grand Prairie, Texas. Selena's parents divorced when she was five. She lived with her mom. Selena's mom later remarried. In 2013, Selena became a big sister.

Selena and her mom attend events together.

GRAND PRAIRIE, TEXAS

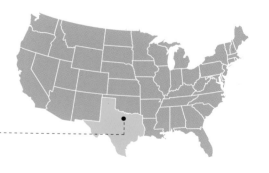

GETTING INTO ACTING

When Selena was growing up, her mom acted in plays. Selena liked to watch her mom *rehearse*. She decided that she wanted to be an actress, too.

....

Selena has won awards for her acting (left) and her music videos (right).

Selena got her first part when she was about 10. She was on the TV show *Barney & Friends* for two years. After *Barney*, Selena got small parts in movies and commercials.

Selena always loved to sing, act, and dance in front of the cameras.

THE BIG TIME

In 2004, Selena was chosen to be on the Disney Channel. At first, Selena got small parts on Disney shows. In 2007, she became a star on the TV show *Wizards of Waverly Place*. The show was filmed in Los Angeles, California. So Selena and her mom moved there.

Selena played a young wizard named Alex on TV.

In 2008, Selena started the band Selena Gomez & the Scene. The band's first album came out in 2009. Selena's first big-screen movie, *Ramona and Beezus*, came out in 2010. Selena has won many Kids' Choice and Teen Choice Awards for her acting and singing.

Selena's movie Ramona and Beezus *is based on a famous children's book.*

OFF THE SCREEN

When she is not working, Selena spends time with her family and friends. She loves playing with her six dogs and surfing. Selena also helps raise money for the *United Nations Children's Fund* (UNICEF).

....

Selena got all her dogs from animal shelters.

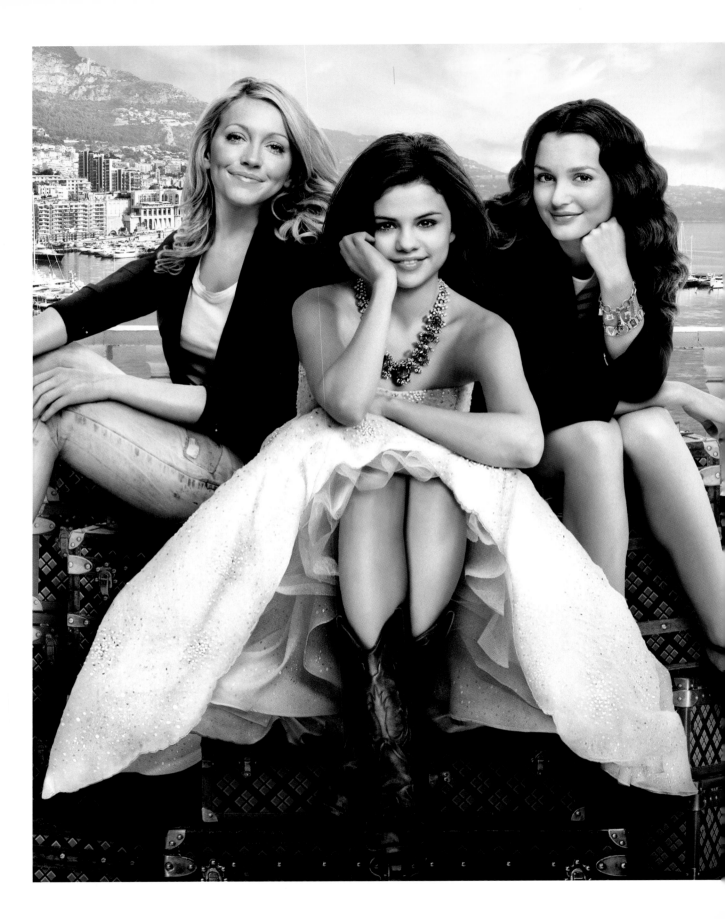

WHAT IS NEXT?

In 2013, Selena made her first **solo** album. She hoped to make more albums in the future. She also planned to keep acting and to **produce** movies. Selena's work is likely to keep fans cheering for years to come!

....

In 2011, Selena had fun acting and singing in the movie Monte Carlo *(left).*

WHAT SELENA SAYS ABOUT ...

AUDITIONING FOR *BARNEY*

"I was definitely nervous; I was very shy when I was younger.... It was scary—and those situations are still scary for me—but it was fun at the same time."

BEING CONFIDENT

"You can't think that you're not as good as anyone else."

MUSIC TOURS

"Touring is the best experience. My fans mean the world to me."

GLOSSARY

produce to take charge of and pay for the making of a movie

rehearse to practice for a performance such as a play or concert

solo done by one person

United Nations Children's Fund a group that gives healthcare, food, and education to needy children around the world

READ MORE

Tieck, Sarah. *Selena Gomez*. Edina, Minn.: Abdo, 2009.

Vaughan, Jenny. *Selena Gomez*. Mankato, Minn.: Sea-to-Sea, 2013.

Williams, Zella. *Selena Gomez: Actress and Singer*. New York: PowerKids Press, 2011.

WEBSITES

Selena Gomez
http://selenagomez.com/
This is Selena's own website, with news, pictures, and videos.

Selena Gomez Biography
http://www.people.com/people/selena_gomez/
This site has information about Selena's life and many pictures, too.

INDEX

PUBLISHED BY Creative Education
P.O. Box 227, Mankato, Minnesota 56002
Creative Education is an imprint of The Creative Company
www.thecreativecompany.us

DESIGN AND PRODUCTION BY Christine Vanderbeek
PRINTED IN the United States of America

PHOTOGRAPHS BY Alamy (AF archive, Pictorial Press Ltd), Corbis (Christopher Ameruoso/Splash News, RD/Orchon/Retna Ltd., RD/Xavier Collin/Retna Digit/Retna Ltd.), Getty Images (FilmMagic, STAN HONDA/AFP, Jason LeVeris/FilmMagic, Craig Sjodin/Disney Channel), iStockphoto (colevineyard, Pingebat), Shutterstock (Randy Miramontez, s_bukley)

LIBRARY OF CONGRESS CATALOGING-IN-PUBLICATION DATA
Bodden, Valerie.
Selena Gomez / Valerie Bodden.
p. cm. — (The big time)
Includes index.
Summary: An elementary introduction to the life, work, and popularity of Selena Gomez, an American pop singer and actress known for her work on children's shows and such songs as "Come & Get It."

ISBN 978-1-60818-498-9
1. Gomez, Selena, 1992– —Juvenile literature. 2. Actors—United States—Biography—Juvenile literature. 3. Singers—United States—Biography—Juvenile literature. I. Title.
PN2287.G585B64 2014
791.4302'8092—dc23 [B]   2014000252

CCSS: RI.1.1, 2, 3, 4, 5, 6, 7; RI.2.1, 2, 5, 6, 7; RI.3.1, 5, 7, 8; RI.4.3, 5; RF.1.1, 3, 4; RF.2.3, 4

FIRST EDITION
9 8 7 6 5 4 3 2 1

Note: Every effort has been made to ensure that the websites listed above are suitable for children, that they have educational value, and that they contain no inappropriate material. However, because of the nature of the Internet, it is impossible to guarantee that these sites will remain active indefinitely or that their contents will not be altered.